The Sovereign Efficacy of Divine Providence

by Urian Oakes
with chapters by C. Matthew McMahon

Copyright Information

The Sovereign Efficacy of Divine Providence, by Urian Oakes, with chapters by C. Matthew McMahon
Edited by Therese B. McMahon

Copyright ©2020 by Puritan Publications and A Puritan's Mind™

Some language and grammar have been updated from the original manuscript. Any change in wording or punctuation has not changed the intent or meaning of the original authors, and has been made to aid the modern reader.

Published by Puritan Publications
A Ministry of A Puritan's Mind™ in Crossville, TN.
www.apuritansmind.com
www.puritanpublications.com

All rights reserved. No part of this publication may be reproduced, stored in a retrieval system or transmitted in any form by any means, electronic, mechanical, photocopy, recording or otherwise, without the prior permission of the publisher, except as provided by USA copyright law.

This Print Edition, 2020
Electronic Edition, 2020
Manufactured in the United States of America

ISBN: 978-1-62663-359-9
eISBN: 978-1-62663-358-2

Table of Contents

A Brief Note on God's Sovereignty 4

Meet Urian Oakes 8

To the Reader 12

Part 1: The Text 17

Part 2: The Doctrine 25

Part 3: Time and Chance 38

Part 4: God's Determination 43

Part 5: Of Instruction – Use 1 51

Part 6: Of Instruction – Use 2 56

Part 7: Of Instruction – Use 3 58

Part 8: Of Exhortation – Use 4 63

Part 9: Conclusion 82

Other Helpful Works from Puritan Publications 87

A Brief Note on God's Sovereignty
by C. Matthew McMahon, Ph.D., Th.D.

I interject a *reminder* here, as an introduction to this helpful work by Urian Oakes. It is a further support to merely remind you, the reader, that God is the sovereign God of the universe, and that all things fall out according to *his* supreme rule, whether that is in something as difficult as the coronavirus, or a lost job, or poor finances, or *anything* that happens in your life or my life. The rub here, is that people *do not like it* when preachers say, "God is the sovereign God of the universe, and all things fall out according to his supreme rule, *no matter what they are.*" It's that little phrase, "no matter what they are" where people *bock*. They do not like, or cannot accept, that God governs *everything*, and in his sovereign efficacy of ruling all things by his supreme power, that divine providence is truly under his watchful and ordering eye. Consider, briefly, the *following:*

The Bible states that God is sovereign over the entire universe, (Psa. 103:19; Rom. 8:28; Eph. 1:11), God is sovereign over all of nature, (Psa. 135:6-7; Matt. 5:45;

6:25-30), God is sovereign over angels and Satan, (Psa. 103:20-21; Job 1:12), God is sovereign over nations, (Psa. 47:7-9; Dan. 2:20-21; 4:34-35), God is sovereign over human beings, (1 Sam. 2:6-7; Gal. 1:15-16), God is sovereign over animals, (Psa. 104:21-30; 1 Kings 17:4-6), God is sovereign over things that seem to be an accident, (Prov. 16:33; John 1:7; Matt. 10:29), God is sovereign over free acts of men, (Exod. 3:21; 12:25-36; Ezek. 7:27), God is sovereign over sinful acts of men and Satan, (2 Sam. 24:1; 1 Chron. 21:1; Gen 45:5; 50:20). Since the Bible plainly teaches these truths, all good Christians formulate their theological ideas about God's will and actions in the context of God's good pleasure, will, and sovereign providence. This truth of the biblical doctrine of the sovereign efficacy of his divine providence permeates *every* aspect of the Christian life. These are truths that Mr. Oakes will lay out clearly and precisely.

Where God reveals himself, the Christian is to listen. Those that do not listen to the revelation of God in the manner in which God has provided it to fallen men are in fact *rejecting* the voice of the Creator. This rejection of God's voice is practical atheism, a rebellion against him. Augustine says as a preacher, such people "will not listen to us, they hate the Gospel itself."[1] May such people listen closely to the words of Mr. Oakes, that they might be placed on sound ground, and sure footing, as he expounds the Scriptures.

Everything in the sphere of creation is set under the utter sovereignty of God and his divine providence. God regulates everything, all the time, and all things are under his power. There is no autonomous atom running around the universe that is not under the direct control and power of the sovereignty of God. If there were, this one rogue atom could, in some way, thwart the will of God and confound God's purposes or plan. But there are *no* autonomous entities of any kind since every atom, everything created, is under the *direct* control of God. This extends even into the farthest reaches of darkness and sinful acts. Even the acts of darkness, and the acts of wicked men, are subject to the will of God so that they cannot do anything that God has not willed or decreed. God does not *make* men sin, but he so manipulates the order of the world and all its circumstances that his sovereign power extends to *everything*. Even acts that are contrary to God's word are accomplished because

---

[1] Phillip Schaff, *Nicene & Post-Nicene Fathers*, s.1, v.06 (16), Augustine, Sermons on the Selected Lessons of the Gospel, Sermon 79 (Albany, Oregon: 1996) 1073.

God's secret counsel ordained that they would be done. For example, God condemns *murder* in his word, but men *still* murder. They murder because God decreed that they would murder in his secret counsel. Those murders in some way will ultimately glorify him in his justice and righteousness, and may ultimately be used for the good of the saints. Take for example, the murder of Jesus Christ upon the cross. God commands that "thou shalt not murder." But the Jews *murdered* Jesus Christ. Was this planned before the foundations of the world? This was God's sovereign efficacious divine providence working itself in time for the good of his church. And *thank goodness* God ordained such a murder to take place for our salvation! And so here, listen carefully to the sound instruction of Mr. Oakes for spiritual wisdom and soul-enriching benefits, who precisely exhibits the power of God in his sovereign efficacy of divine providence over the whole world for our good and his glory.

In Christ's Sovereign Power,
C. Matthew McMahon, Ph.D., Th.D.
From my study, May, 2020.

Meet Urian Oakes
Edited by C. Matthew McMahon, Ph.D., Th.D.

Urian Oakes (1631–1681) was a New England divine, originally born in England in 1631 or possibly 1632. When he was a child, he left England with his father to go to Massachusetts. He graduated at Harvard College in 1649.[2]

While in America he married Ruth, daughter of a well-known nonconformist minister, William Ames. Oakes returned to England during the time of the Commonwealth, and obtained a pastorate in Titchfield. From there he was ejected in 1662. His wife died in 1669. Two years later a deputation sent over to England to find a minister for the vacant church of Cambridge in Massachusetts and chose Oakes. He commenced his pastoral labors in November of 1671, and soon after he became one of the governors of Harvard College.[3] The college was in a difficult situation owing to the general dissatisfaction of the students with their president, Leonard Hoar. The same feeling was in some measure shared and countenanced by certain of the governors,

---

[2] Calamy and Palmer, ii. 280
[3] Harvard was originally founded to raise up Gospel ministers.

and among them was Oakes. He and other of his colleagues resigned, and, in spite of the entreaties of the general court of overseers, would not withdraw their resignation until Hoar himself vacated the presidency on March 15, 1675. The vacancy thus created was filled by the appointment of Oakes. He, however, would only accept it provisionally; but after discharging the duties of the office for four years, in 1679 he consented to accept the full appointment, and held it until his death on July 25, 1681. Edmund Calamy states that Oakes was noted for "the uncommon sweetness of his temper," and in New England he was greatly beloved by his congregation and popular with all who came in contact with him.

His writings are "The Victorious Christian Soldier," "The Sovereign Efficacy of Divine Providence,"[4] three sermons—two preached at the annual election of the artillery company in 1672 and 1676, and the third at

---

[4] *The Sovereign Efficacy of Divine Providence,* preached September 10, 1677, by Mr. Urian Oakes, the late (and still to be Lamented) Reverend Pastor of the Church of Christ in Cambridge, and Learned President of Harvard College. Psa. 29:10, "The Lord sitteth upon the flood: yea the Lord sitteth King forever." Isa. 41:14-15, "Fear not thou worm of Jacob. I will help thee, saith the Lord, and thy Redeemer. Thou shalt thresh the Mountains." Rom. 11:36, "For of him, and through him, and to him, are all things, to whom be glory for ever. Amen." (Boston, MA: s.n. 1682).

the election of representatives in 1673—and a monody in English verse (Cambridge, 1677) on the death of Thomas Shepard, minister of the church in Charlestown. Mr. Tyler describes Oakes' one surviving effort in poetry as "not without some mechanical defects," yet, on the whole, Oakes' power, dignity, and directness raise him far above the contemporary verse-writers of New England.

Oakes stands out far more conspicuously above his contemporaries by the merits of his prose. In substance his sermons wholly break through any mere formalities of Calvinism. They are intensely human, alike in their treatment of moral problems and their application of scriptural examples. The preacher is throughout a vigorous moralist, full of public spirit. The style is concise and precise (as many of his theological puritan counterparts), yet free from conceits or forced antithesis, and capable of rising into real dignity and eloquence. The purity and elegance of his Latin are proved by an example preserved in Cotton Mather's "Magnalia."

For more information, see:

Savage's *Genealogical Dict. of New England*; Cotton Mather's *Magnalia*; Tyler's *History of American Literature*; Holmes's *History of Cambridge*; Peirce's *History of Harvard University*, (pp. 44–46); Appleton's *Cyclop. of American Biogr.* Volume iv, 548; Hutchinson's *History of Massachusetts*.

To the Reader

Christian Reader,

What you are here presented with, is a part of the pious and profitable labors of that faithful ambassador of Christ, Mr. Urian Oakes. Who, having served his generation by the will of God, in the Gospel of his Son, and being willing to exchange this for a better world, did in his passage here, let fall, and (as something of Elijah with his mantle) leave behind him this work, with other useful fruits of his well-studied, and elaborate meditations. By this, and an amiable, exemplary, instructive, well-ordered Christian conversation, he being dead, yet speaks.

It will be a sin, and shame to such as knew and had opportunity to enjoy him, to forget how great a price we had in our hands, while for a few years, we were permitted by him, who walking amidst the golden candlesticks, holds the stars in his right hand, to have the heat, and help of such a burning, and shinning a light. We shall also be blameworthy, and guilty of a greatly-provoking evil, if we do not mind how much we have lost, and are tremendously weakened by the fall of so principal a pillar; and what cause we have to lament, that by an immature, and (as to us) a *too* early a death, and dissolution, so bright-shining a star is now no more visible. He has been removed and taken up to shine in a higher orb. It is doubtless a sad omen, and signal of a near approaching night of blackness, and darkness, when our heavenly Father calls to put his children to bed. The removing and taking away of shepherds, and principal men from a people, what is it, but a casting down their pillars, a plucking up their stakes, a bereaving them of their chariots and horsemen, and leaving them without their defense and strength. Do not let an unaffected, senseless stupidity under that late dreadful dispensation of a provoked God, give occasion to take up against us that sad complaint.

> Isa. 57:1, "The righteous perisheth, and no man layeth it to heart: and merciful men (or men of godliness) are taken away, none considering," *etc.*

Surely, from the going away of such, survivors may conclude that evil is coming. Let Noah be shut into the Ark; Lot removed; and zealous tender-hearted Josiah laid to sleep in his bed of dust. And the appointed executioners of God's direful displeasure, elements and enemies, shall immediately set on and assault to their confusion, a people ripe for ruin. O! that we were wise to lay to heart and consider!

The eminent worth, and rare accomplishments of the (now blessed) author, none but such as did not know him, or envied him, can, or will deny. The rare beauties, and sweets of nature, learning, and grace which the great God had endowed, and adorned him with, were such, and so attractive, that nothing but unacquaintance disingenuity, and prejudice could secure from being captivated, and held fast in the pleasant bonds of love, and delight. Had all the art, and grace he was filled, and furnished with, been tuned up into an ill-scented cask, tainted with haughtiness, peevishness, and vanity; their flavor, and delightful sweetness would have been lost in a nauseous unpleasancy. What he was to myself, I cannot without renewing my grief, express. I shall only say, he was (what is rare, and hard to be found in this lower world) a delightful, loving, profitable, fast and faithful friend. Being gone, I cannot forbear following with David's elegy, and complaint for his beloved Jonathan; "I am distressed for thee my dear brother, very pleasant hast thou been unto me." But, "the Lord lives, and blessed be my Rock; and let the God of my salvation be exalted." Amen.

The design of this work, as left by the author written with his own hand, now published in print, is to vindicate the glory of the blessed God in his all-ruling, wonder-working providence as sovereignly disposing the issues and events of all human counsels, and affairs. The most High rules and reigns, (as to his declarative glory) even from his dearest and best servants. For they are clogged, and cumbered with the remains of ignorance, atheism, unbelief, carnal reason, *etc.* While we are too intent in gazing on the living creatures, and the dreadful wheels of Ezekiel, (which by their swift, and whirling motion do often raise a cloud of dust) we soon lose the sight of him who sits above on the throne, overruling, and working all things according to the counsel of his own will. We are apt to be too fearful, and distrustful in our entrance on, and too forgetful of God in the issues of great and doubtful affairs; quicker of sight to discover a host of Aramites, than to discern an army of angels, like him in 2 Kings 6:15-17, and more ready to give too much to creatures, than to ascribe to

To the Reader

God his due, (Judges 7:2–6). Prevention of, and help against evils, so prejudicial to ourselves and dishonorable to God, was the aim of the author in this ensuing seasonable, and serious discourse. It is worthy to be perused by all to whose hands it may come. The face of affairs, in the times now passing over our heads, is such, and so agreeable to what truth himself foretold in Luke 21:25-26, as proves it (beyond dispute) needful to be perused, prayed over, and improved, to a securing to ourselves comfort; and to the blessed God his ever due glory. That it may be so, is the unfeigned wish of him who is...

Thine in the Lord Jesus,
JOHN SHERMAN

Part 1: The Text

Eccl. 9:11, "I returned, and saw under the sun, that the race is not to the swift, nor the battle to the strong, neither yet bread to the wise, nor yet riches to men of understanding, nor yet favor to men of skill; but time, and chance happeneth to them all."

This book of Ecclesiastes is generally, and probably conceived to be a penitential discourse of Solomon, in his old age, for the satisfaction of the church and people of God concerning his own repentance. It is for their instruction and direction, how to enjoy the best good of the things of this world, and yet not to make them their best good, but estimate them as vanity in this respect, and to steer a direct course towards that which is the last end of man, the glory of God and his fruition, in the way of *fearing God, and keeping his commandments*. As David after his great fall penned his penitential psalm (Psalm 51) so it is rationally conjectured that Solomon, his son, being at last thoroughly awakened out of his sensuality, security, and idolatrous courses, or connivances and tolerations, by those great adversaries, Hadad, Rezon, and Jeroboam (of whom you read in 1 Kings 11:14, *etc.*) that God stirred up against him, penned this book of Ecclesiastes, and left it (according to the counsel of God) for a standing monument of his public confession of, and hearty repentance for all his errors, and miscarriages. The general scope of this book, is to show us in which the chief good of man consists; which was the great inquiry of the philosophers of old; about which they had endless opinions and discourses, and could never hit the mark, nor arrive at thorough satisfaction. This is because they lacked the light, and direction of the word, and Spirit of God. Solomon plainly tells us, that the happiness of man consists in the fear, and favor, and fruition of God. It is not in the enjoyment of the honors, profits, or pleasures of this world; or any good thing under the sun. And because man, having by the fall lost God, is turned away to the creature; and as it is originally inlaid in his nature to desire happiness, so it is the bent and inclination of his corrupt nature to pursue it and seek for it in the creature, and good things of this life. Therefore, he is very large and elaborate in discoursing the vanity of all these things, and their insufficiency to make a man blessed, or to make any real contribution towards the essential happiness of man, being never made to be the chief good of man, nor proportioned and suited to the condition of the soul of man, and being made subject to vanity, the greatest vanity! As they were made for man and put into his covenant, and so fell with him under the curse, upon his apostasy from God. The large experience this wise man had of created things, the many proofs and experiments, and curious critical enquiries he had made into the nature, and use of sublunary, or subsolary enjoyments, together with the infallible conduct of the Spirit of God, advantaged him to discourse feelingly, and accurately, as well as largely from point to point concerning the huge vanity of all things under the sun. A great part of the book is spent on this subject. Among other vanities that fall under his observation, this was one and not the least, that men of greatest sufficiency in any course, or kind, meet with many unexpected disappointments in their undertakings. This he declares in the words of my text. Concerning the settling the connection of these words, expositors are not at perfect agreement among themselves. Some apprehend this to be an argument of the Epicureans, by which they would demonstrate that all things in the world are rolled up and down, tumbled and tossed about by mere chance, and fall out as it may happen, uncertainly and fortuitously: because *the race is not to the swift, nor the battle to the strong, etc.* But the ablest men are often crossed in their designs, and defeated of their ends and hopes by these and those intervening accidents. Here they deny the wise, overruling, all-disposing providence of God; and I do not know what imaginary blind fortune they cling to as the predominant deity in the world. But there seems to be no necessity of fixing on such an exposition and accommodation of the words; considering that they may well admit of a better, and more savory construction.

Others think that Solomon has respect here to what he had discoursed before, concerning the unsearchable and uncontrollable providence of God, chapter 8:16-17 and chapter 9:1-2. And whereas he had said there, that *the righteous, and the wise and their works are in the hand of God*, he now shows the truth of that assertion by an induction of particulars.

Others conceive it is a correction of that precept in verses 7-9 of this chapter, concerning the leading a pleasant, and merry life in the free, and comfortable use of outward blessings; which is here cautioned, and corrected by this consideration, that there is a great uncertainty of events, nor do things always succeed according to a rational expectation. This renders it apparent that no man is secure of the perpetuity of his earthly happiness, or assured of the enjoyment of these comforts, and of an even course of prosperity, without many troublesome rubs, and disappointments.

Others judge he has respect to the words immediately preceding verse 10. Where he advises us, *to do what we have to do, with all our might*, while life, and working time continues.[5] And except anyone should therefore presume on a necessity that all things should succeed to him according to his abilities, and endeavors, he subjoins this seasonable admonition, that we should not trust to our own sufficiency, and industry in the management of any business, to which there is no sure entail of success. Instead, we should depend on, and attribute *all* to the gracious concurrence, free favor, and blessing of God.

But whatever may be conjectured about the connection of the words, it is evident that Solomon here acquaints us with a great vanity under the sun, which he had before intimated, when he said, "all things are alike to all, and there is one event to the righteous, and to the wicked, the good and the bad," and here amplifies, and

---

[5] Vid. Voet. *Select disput. Theol.* Par. 4. p. 739.

adds, that swift, and slow, strong, and weak, wise and foolish, have many times the same success; and men of the greatest sufficiency, as well as others, are often disappointed. This Solomon returned and saw *under the sun*, that is, when he took a view of the frame, and posture, and condition of human affairs, among other vanities which he turned his eyes on, this was one over and above the rest, a most unexpected vanity, which he considered over and over, that events do not always answer the abilities, and endeavors of men, and succeed according to their expectations. The vanity which Solomon discovered, and considered, and here acquaints us with, is, that it is not in the power of the ablest men, or best accomplished for action, to effect their designs, or *praestare eventum*, that which is secure, and warrant the event and success of their undertakings. This is, 1. argued, and proved by the induction of five instances in particular, to which many more may by parity of reason be added.

    He says, "the race is not to the swift." It is not always in the power of the swiftest footman to evade danger, or win the prize by running. He says, "nor is the battle to the strong." The victory is not determined, or the decision of the war always made on the side of the strongest and most valiant of men. He says, "nor yet bread to the wise." Many wise men are not able to get their bread, or livelihood in the world. "...nor riches to men of understanding." Many understanding men do not have any success in their endeavors to gather riches and get estates. "...nor favor to men of skill." Many times, the most skillful artists, and artificers, and the best accomplished persons find little favor and acceptation among men, how deserving, and ingenious whatsoever they may be.

2. Illustrated by the antithesis of a different, and the true cause of the determination of successes and events, signified in those words, "but time and chance happeneth to them all," by which we are not to understand that the determination of events is reduced and referred to mere chance and fortune, as the Epicurean philosophers imagined. But that the counsel and providence of God disposes and orders out all successes, or frustrations of second causes, casting in sometimes such unexpected impediments and obstructions, as defeat the labors and hopes of men of the greatest sufficiency. Which, though they seem wholly casual and fortuitous emergencies, (and are so indeed to men themselves), yet they are governed by the

secret counsel and effectual providence of God. The sum is this, that no man, no matter how accomplished they are, is master of events, or absolute determiner of the issues of his own actings and endeavors. But the sovereign counsel and the providence of God orders time and all things to be an effectual furtherance, or hindrance of the designs of all men, as seems good in his sight.

Part 2: The Doctrine

The observation is this ... DOCTRINE: That the successes and events of undertakings and affairs are not infallibly determined by men's greatest sufficiency, or secondary causes; but by the counsel and providence of God ordering and governing time and chance according to his own good pleasure.

I have endeavored to comprise and grasp the substance of Solomon's intendment, in this doctrinal conclusion. And I will explain and demonstrate its truth (as God shall help) in the following propositions.

Proposition 1. Second causes may have a sufficiency in their kind, to produce these and those effects. They have a liability, a congruous disposition, or an aptness, yes, a kind of sufficiency in order to put forth this and that act, and gives existence to these and those effects. It is not indeed an absolute and universal sufficiency (which can be affirmed of none but him that is all sufficient and omnipotent) but a limited sufficiency, or a sufficiency in their kind, and order. The sun shines, the fire burns, as that which is combustible. The rational creature to act or effect this or that in a way of counsel, and with freedom of will; the swift, to run;

the strong and valiant, and well-instructed soldier, to fight well; the wise man, to get his bread to gather riches, to gain acceptance among those with whom he has to do. This is no more than to say, that created agents and second causes, may have the active power and virtue of causes, all that is requisite on their parts in order to the production of their peculiar and appropriate effects, all that sufficiency that dependent beings, and second causes are capable of. And indeed, it belongs to the infinite wisdom and goodness of God to furnish his creatures with sufficient ability for the operations and effects he has made them for. And so, he did at first, when he made everything good in its kind; and whatever defect there is now in this respect, it is the fruit and punishment of sin. Though God is able to give being to things in an immediate way, yet it is his pleasure in the course of his providence to use means, and to produce many things by the mediation and agency of second causes, and so gives causal virtue and ability to these and those things in order to the producing of such and such effects. It is a good observation, that the lord is pleased, not through any defect of power in himself but out of the abundance of his goodness to communicate causal power and virtue to his creatures, and to honor them with that dignity that they may be his instruments, by which he will produce these and those effects. By which he takes them, as it were, into partnership and fellowship with himself in the way of his providential efficiency, that they may be under-workers to, yes, co-workers with himself. Here he gives them an aptitude and sufficiency in their kind in order to their respective operations and effects: though some have a greater aptitude and sufficiency than others. But without some degree of such sufficiency, nothing can deserve the name of a cause; the very essence of this consists in its power, virtue and ability to produce an effect. A cause cannot be a cause without an active power, or sufficiency to give being to this or that effect.

Proposition 2. The successes, and events of affairs and undertakings do ordinarily depend in some respects on the sufficiency of second causes. I do not say in the observation; nor is it the meaning of Solomon, that successes and events of affairs and undertakings do not depend at all in an ordinary course, on the sufficiency of second causes. For this were to deny and destroy their causality, and to make nothing of their efficiency. Second causes have their peculiar influence into their effects, and contribute something to their existence.

And to assert the contrary, were to say that causes are no causes, and to speak a flat contradiction. This would be to suppose that the Lord has set up an order and course in nature, in vain; and given to second causes a sufficiency in their kind, for action, to no purpose; and to deny the ordinary providence of God, which is that by which the Lord observes the order which he has set, and that course of nature which is originally of his own appointment, by which one thing depends on, and receives being from another. Sometimes the Lord is pleased on great and important occasions, to leave the ordinary road of providence, and act beyond and above the usual, stated course of things, and not to concur with, and shine on the endeavors of created agents, so as to crown them with that success which according to an ordinary course of providence, might be rationally expected. Yet, it is not to be imagined that he should ordinarily dispense with the course, and methods of his ordinary providence. For why then should it be called *ordinary?* God who is the Lord of Hosts, the great leader commander and ruler of nature, not only permits, but also effectually commands and causes his whole militia, ordinarily, to move and act according to their natures and natural properties respectively, without countermanding them, or turning them out of their way. For (as I remember one argues) he will not show such a dislike to his own workmanship, as ordinarily to cross the order, and alter the course he has set in the world.

Therefore, the meaning of the text is not, that swiftness conduces nothing to the winning of the race, or strength, to the winning of the battle, or wisdom and understanding, to the getting of bread and riches; or prudence, art, or skill, to get favor and good will of princes, or people. Nor, that the race is never to the swift, or the battle never to the strong; no nor yet, that the race is not more frequently to the swift, and the battle usually to the strong, *etc.* For the Lord most ordinarily awards success to causes of greatest sufficiency, rather than disappointment and defeat. Otherwise, it would be a very heartless, if not a foolish thing (in the eye of reason) to use means, or to think to get the race by swiftness, or bread by labor and diligence, or favor by dexterous and prudent behavior; or learning, by study and industry; or to win the battle by good conduct, and courage, and numbers of men. Yes, then wisdom would not be better than folly nor strength more desirable than weakness; nor diligence more beneficial and available than idleness, and sitting still.

This, therefore, is evident, that the issues and events of undertakings do in some respect, ordinarily, depend on the sufficiency of second causes; insomuch as the greatest probability of success (according to an ordinary providence, and in the eye of reason) is ordinarily on the side of causes that are most sufficient in their kind of efficiency.

Proposition 3. Second causes, though of greatest sufficiency in their kind, do not have the certain determination of successes and events in their own hands; but may be frustrated and disappointed.

Though the successes and events of undertakings ordinarily depend on the sufficiency of second causes; yet they are not infallibly determined by them. Created agents do not have events in their own hands, but may be disappointed. They cannot warrant the events of their undertakings, or success of their counsels and endeavors, but may be defeated of their hopes and expectations. In this way no man has the absolute command of the issue and success of his own undertakings. He may be sure of this or that event, if the Lord promises it to him, or reveals it to be his pleasure to give such success to such endeavors. But he cannot be secured of it from, or by any sufficiency of his own. He may, as a wise man, foresee and say, what in an ordinary course of providence is rationally to be expected; but cannot warrant the success of his undertakings, or carve out what event he pleases, to himself. His prudence, and providence, and diligence, and sufficiency for action, cannot assure him of the event, or determine the success on his side. And there is that demonstration of it, that created agents of the greatest sufficiency, are sometimes disappointed. Two things I would say *here:*

    1. Agents of greatest sufficiency are subject to disappointment, as well (I do not say, as much, or as ordinarily and often, but as well) as agents of less sufficiency. The ablest men in any kind may miss of the success they expect, as well as weaker men. That men of great sufficiency in this or that way, may be defeated of their ends and hopes, Solomon from his own experience, assures us, in the text. And who is it that on his own observation cannot set his seal to what he asserts? He gives five instances. 1. The race is not to the swift. Not profitable, or successful to him always; but sometimes pernicious, and destructive. Many good runners run himself into mischief and ruin. Thus Ashael, that is said to be as light of foot as a wild roe, ran after Abner so fast, that he lost his life in that overhasty pursuit (2 Sam.

2:18–23). There are times when men that are swift would run from danger, and cannot. They have neither power to run, nor success in attempting it, (Jer. 46:6). Sometimes the flight perishes from the swift, and he that is swift of foot, or that rides the horse, though it be at full speed, cannot deliver himself, (Amos 2:14-15). It is not absolutely in the power of the swiftest man to escape danger, or win the prize by running.

2. The battle is not to the strong. There is in *bello alea*, the chance of war, as they use to speak. There is, as it were, a kind of lottery, a great uncertainty in war. Great armies are sometimes defeated by small and inconsiderable forces; the great host of Midian, by Gideon's three hundred men; the garrison of the philistines by Jonathan, and his armor-bearer. This has been often observed in the world. Sometimes strong and valiant men are overthrown by those that are in strength far inferior to them; great Goliath, by little David. Well might David say, as Psalm 33:16-17, "There is no king saved by the multitude of a host: a mighty man is not delivered by much strength. A horse is a vain thing for safety: neither shall he deliver any by his great strength."

There are times, when "the mighty ones are beaten down," (Jer. 46:5). And, "the mighty cannot deliver himself, or the strong strengthen himself; but the courageous among the mighty is put to flight," (Amos 2:14-16). Sometimes the strong melt like water at approaching danger, and the stouthearted are spoiled and sleep their sleep, and the men of might cannot find their hands, "to make the least defense, or resistance," (Psa. 76:5).

3. The bread is not to the wise. Wise men are not able to get their livelihood, but have much *ado* to make a shift to get a bare subsistence in the world; and, it may be, are forced to beg for it, or be beholding to the charity of others. There have been strange instances of very wise, and worthy persons, that have been reduced to such a condition. Some of you know the famous story, *date obolum,* or (as others have it) *panem belisario.* David was put to beg his bread of Nabal, (1 Sam. 25). And Paul was often in hunger and thirst, (2 Cor. 11:27).

4. Riches are not to men of understanding. Sometimes indeed, wise men get estates and gather riches; and one would think they should be best accomplished for it: and yet it so falls out, that some understanding men cannot thrive in the world and grow rich, notwithstanding all their endeavors. So it is, that many men of great understanding and rational

forecastings and contrivances to gather wealth, though they lay out their parts and their hearts this way, and would be rich, yet they cannot; but are strangely defeated. You read of the poor wise man, (Eccl. 9:15). Many men of great understandings are too wise, and of too great spirits to labor after wealth; or if they do, their designs are unsuccessful.

5. Favor is not to men of skill. Many very wise, and knowing, and skillful men, and experienced in affairs, and prudent also in their deportment, yet cannot get, or keep the favor of princes or people. Some expositors on the place, instance in Joseph, that was envied, and hated, and sold by his brethren, and also lost the favor of Potiphar (though he managed the affairs of his house prudently and prosperously, and deserved well at his hands) and was cast into prison by him. David, that was hated and persecuted by Saul; Daniel, that was cast into the lion's den, though an excellent spirit was found in him, and great prudence and faithfulness in managing the affairs of the empire; and before that, though he had been in great favor and esteem in Nebuchadnezzar's time, yet afterwards in the reign of Belshazzar, he lived obscure, and as it were buried at court, as Mr. Cartwright gathers from Dan.

5:11-13. Many wise, and learned, and ingenious men cannot get the favor of men, or keep it, when they have. The poor wise man delivered the city, and yet no man remembered that same poor man, (Eccl. 9:15). Belisarius (whom I mentioned before) was a most prudent, experienced, faithful general under the Emperor Justinian, that had won him many battles, reduced many cities and countries to his obedience and approved himself for a most loyal, and worthy subject, and yet after all his services, even in that emperor's time was through envy, falsely accused, for as appears by the story, had his eyes put out, and was forced to stand daily in the temple of Sophia, where he held out his wooden dish, begging his bread, and using those words, "give a little bread to Belisarius," whom his virtue and valor has raised; and envy depressed, and cast down again.

Other scripture testimonies and instances, besides those in the text, might be produced, if it were needful. But every observing man's experience may furnish him with demonstrations of this truth, that agents of greatest sufficiency among men are subject to disappointments, as well as those of less sufficiency.

Again, 2. agents of little, or no sufficiency, succeed sometimes in their undertakings; when those of greater sufficiency, miscarry and meet with disappointment. There are many times one event to both as Solomon speaks in Eccl. 9:2, when the ablest agents are frustrated, as well as the weakest. And there is sometimes a better event to weaker agents, and instruments; they prosper in their way, when abler men are disappointed. The race is sometimes to the slow, and the swift lose the prize. The battle is sometimes to the weak; and the strong are put to flight. As we have many instances both in scripture and common history. Weak and simple people have bread enough sometimes, when wise men are in want of their daily bread. Nabal had good store, when David was hard put to it. Men of shallow heads grow rich and get great estates, when men of understanding can thrive at no hand. Solomon tells us of the poor wise man; and our Savior in that parable, (Luke 12:16-20), tells us of a rich fool. It is ordinarily seen in the world, that the thriving men in estates, are none of the most understanding and judicious. Many a man has this world-craft, that yet is a man of no deep or solid understanding. So, many weak, worthless, ignorant, empty persons find favor with princes and people. When men of skill, and learning, and great worth are neglected and despised. This is an evil under the sun, and an error that proceeds from the ruler, a great miscarriage in government, that "folly is set in great dignity" (fools are favored and advanced) and the rich, (*i.e.* men of rich endowments for wisdom and piety), sit in low places, (*i.e.* are depressed and discountenanced). Servants are upon horses, men of poor servile spirits and conditions, are set up and honored, and princes, (i.e. men of great worth), walk as servants on the earth, (Eccl. 10:5-7).

So that it appears plainly, that success does not always wait on the counsels and actions of people of great sufficiency; but they may suffer disappointment, when others are prosperous. This demonstrates that the issues and events of undertakings and affairs are not determined infallibly by the qualifications and accomplishments of created agents, and second causes.

Part 3: Time and Chance

Proposition 4. The defeat and disappointment of agents of great sufficiency in their kind, is from the happening of time and chance to them.

Some read it (and the original will bear it) because, or "for time and chance happens to them all." For an explanation. 1. By time, do not understand barely the duration, or space of time, which has no such determining influence into human affairs. But time so and so circumstanced. Time is sometimes as much as a special season or opportunity, when there is a concurrence of helps, means, and advantages for the furthering the designs and undertakings of men. By *time* sometimes, we are to understand such a nick, or juncture of time, in which there is a coincidence of difficulties, disadvantages, and hindrances to the effecting of any business. And this seems the meaning of Solomon in the text; an adverse or evil time, (Eccl. 9:12). Sometimes the times favor the enterprises of men, sometimes they frown on them. At one time, wise and good men stand up for the defense of their country and liberties of it, and prosper in it; the times favor them, there is a concurrence of all manner of furtherance and advantage. At another time, they may endeavor it, and the times frown upon them, the spirit and humor of the people is degenerated; and they swim against the stream, and are lost in the attempt. And we say, such a man was worthy of better times, had been a brave man, if he had lived in better times, his worth would have been more known and prized, and he would have had better success. So, when the time of judgment on a people, is come, then wrath arises against them without remedy; and then the strong man may fight for the defense of such a country; and the wise man endeavor to deliver the city. But all in vain; they shall miscarry in the undertaking. Aben ezra (as Mercer tells us) refers this to the conjunctions, and aspects of the stars, by which he apprehended these inferior things were governed. We are sure there are certain periods, and revolutions of time, respecting the prosperity, or adversity of nations, countries, cities, churches, families, persons. As time is set to all the successes, so to all the defeats and disappointments of men; and when this time comes, no sufficiency of man can withstand disappointments.

2. By chance, understand contingent and casual events. Many things fall out between the cup, and the lip; or otherwise than expect or imagine, or can possibly

foresee. Some event chops in, and interposes unexpectedly, to cross a man's designs, and defeat his hopes and rational expectations. When Saul and his men were compassing David and his men, and ready to take them, then comes a messenger to Saul, saying, "haste and come: For the Philistines have invaded the land," (1 Sam. 23:27). When Haman had plotted the ruin of the Jews, and brought his design near to an issue, then the king cannot sleep but calls for the book of the records of the Chronicles, and they read to him of the good service of Mordecai, in discovering the treason that was plotted against his person; and one thing falls in after another, to defeat Haman's cruel design, and ruin the whole fabric of his strong built, and almost perfected contrivance. In this sense time and chance happens to men of greatest sufficiency, which they cannot either foresee, (Eccl. 9:12), or prevent, or help themselves against them when they come on them. And hereby their counsels, and undertakings are defeated and ruined sometimes.

Proposition 5. Time and chance, which happens to men in the way of their undertakings, are effectually ordered and governed by the Lord. God is the Lord of time, and orderer, and Governor of all contingences.

Time and chance that further or hinder the designs of men, are under the rule and management of the Lord. His counsel sets the times, appoints the chances; his providence dispenses the times, and frames the chances, that befall men. The Lord has in his own power the dispensation of times, (Eph. 1:10). "...the times and seasons he has put in his own power," (Acts 1:7). He has such a dominion over the times, that, "he changeth times and seasons, according to his own pleasure," (Dan. 2:21). "My times," David says in Psalm 31:15, "are in thy hands." He means the state and condition of his times; his prosperities, and adversities; his successes, and disappointments; and universally, whatever should befall him in the times that should pass over him. Moreover, all the chances that happen to men, as the scripture but now mentioned shows, are in the hand of God. "My times," *i.e.* the chances of my times. No contingency, or emergency, or accident so casual, but it is ordered and governed by the Lord. The arrow that was shot at a venture, and struck Ahab through the joints of his harness, was directed at him by the hand of God. So, in that case of man-slaughter, and killing a man casually, as if a man is hewing wood, and his hand fetches a stroke with the axe, to cut down a tree, and the head slips from the shaft, and strikes on his neighbor, that he dies, (Deut. 19:5), God is said in that case, to, "deliver that man that is slain, into his hand," (Exod. 21:13). God orders that sad event. All casualties in the world, are guided by the steady hand of the great God. David says in Psalm 16:5, "Thou maintainest my lot." The Lord makes and disposes the lot, or chance of every man, whatever it is. He has appointed all times and chances in his eternal counsel; and in time executes accordingly, in the course of his providence.

Part 4: God's Determination

Proposition 6. The great God has the absolute and infallible determination of the successes and events of all the operations and undertakings of created agents and second causes, in his own power. His counsel and sovereign will appoints what they shall be, and his providence (which is not determined by any second cause, but is the determiner of them all) executes all things accordingly. And it must needs be so, if you consider these two *particulars:*

1. God is the absolute first cause, and supreme Lord of all. "Of him, and to him, and through him are all things," (Rom. 11:36). He that understands anything of God indeed, knows this to be a truth. Here we might be large; as they that are acquainted with the doctrine of creation and providence, in conservation and gubernation of all things, will readily apprehend. For here we might show you, that God is the absolute first cause of all the causal power and virtue that is in creatures. He gives them power to act, furnishes them with a sufficiency for their operations. He gives swiftness to the runner; skill, and strength, and courage, to the soldier.

2. That he supports, and continues the active power of the creature. He continues swiftness, wisdom, strength, courage, as he pleases. If he withdraws, everything is gone. The swift is lame, or slow-footed, the strong is weak and timorous, the wise is foolish and drunk, the man of skill, is a mere bungler at anything.

3. That he does by a previous influx excite and stir up, and actuate the active power of the creature, and sets all the wheels going. For the most operative, active created virtue, is not a pure act. But has some potentiality mixed with it; and therefore, cannot put forth itself into action, unless it is set going by the First Cause. And the creature cannot be the absolute first cause of any physical action. "... in him we live, and move," (Acts 17:28).

Again, 4. That he determines and applies second causes to the objects of their actions. When they stand, as it were, *in bivio*, as it is said of Nebuchadnezzar, when he was marching with his army he, "stood at the parting of the way," at the head of the two ways, to use divination, as doubting which way he had best to march, whether to Jerusalem, or some other way, (Ezek. 21:21-22). Then the Lord casts the scale and the lot, and determines them this way, and not another. He does not only stir up second causes to act at large, and set them going, and leave it to their own inclination, whether they shall go, and what they shall do. But he leads them forth, and determines them to this, or that object.

5. That he cooperates, and works jointly with second causes, in producing their effects. As he predetermines second causes, so he concurs with them in their operations. And this predetermination, and concourse is so necessary; that there can be no real effect produced by the creature without it. And it is a truth also, that when God improves second causes for the production of any effect, he so concurs with them, that he does with it most immediately, intimately, and without dependence on these causes by which he acts, produce the entity, or *esse* of the effect. If this is considered, it will appear that created agents, are as it were, God's instruments, that act as they are acted by him; and cannot move of themselves. The busy, bustling, proud Assyrian was this way in Isaiah 10:15.

6. That all the ataxia, disorder, irregularity, moral evil that is found in the actions of rational agents, is by his permission. If it were not the pleasure of God to permit it, no sin should be in the world, nor in the actions of men. Though there is no legal permission, or

allowance of it; (for the law of God forbids it) yet there is a providential permission of it. God could have kept it out of his world.

7. That he limits and sets bounds to the actions of second causes. What they shall do, and how far they shall proceed in this or that way. He set bounds to Satan, when he had commission to afflict Job. He limits, and restrains, the eruptions of the wrath and rage of the church's adversaries, (Psalm 76:10). He sets bounds to the sinful actions of men. He regulates and governs all the actions of second causes, as to time, place, degrees, and all manner of circumstances. He is not the author, but he is the Orderer of sin itself.

8. That he serves himself, and his own ends of all second causes. He makes them all in all their operations subservient to his own designs. And that not only natural, but rational agents, that act by counsel. And not only such of them as are his professed willing servants. Many serve God's ends beside their intentions, and against their wills. "I will do this and that" God says, by the "Assyrian, howbeit he meaneth not so," (Isa. 10:6-7).

Wicked men and devils do God's will against their own will, and besides their intentions. "Ye thought evil against me, Joseph says to his brethren, "but God meant it for good," *etc.*, (Gen. 50:20). God elicits what good he pleases out of the actions of his creatures. Whatever this or that agent proposes to himself, yet God always attains his ends. He serves himself of the very sins of his creatures, and brings good out of them. He makes that which is not *bonum honestum*, to be *bonum conducibile*. And though sin is not good; yet, as God orders the matter, *it is good, in order to many holy ends, that sin should be in the world*, as Augustine observes.

9. That he uses means in themselves unfit, and improves agents of themselves insufficient, to bring about his own purposes and produce marvelous effects. Yes, and it is as easy with him to do anything by weak and insufficient, as by the ablest and most accomplished instruments. "...there is no restraint to the Lord to save by many, or by few," (1 Sam. 14:6). "It is nothing with him to help, whether with many, or with them that have no power," (2 Chron. 14:11). Despicable instruments, sometimes, do great things in his hand.

10. That he renders the aptest means ineffectual, and the undertakings of the most sufficient agents unsuccessful, when he pleases. He has a negative voice upon all the counsels and endeavors, and active power

of the creature. He can stop the sun in its course, and cause it to withdraw its shining; he can give check to the fire, that it shall not burn; and to the hungry lions, that they shall not devour. And he can order it so, that the men of might shall sleep their sleep, and not find their hands. He can break the ranks of the most orderly soldiers, take away courage from the stoutest hearts, send a panic fear into a mighty host, and defeat the counsels of the wisest leaders and conductors. He can blow upon, and blast the likeliest undertakings of the ablest men. In a word, the Lord being the absolute first cause, and supreme Governor of all his creatures, and all their actions; though he has set an order among his creatures, this shall be the cause of that effect, *etc.* Yet he himself is not tied to that order; but interrupts its course when he pleases. The Lord reserves a liberty to himself to interpose, and to umpire matters of success and event, contrary to the law and common rule of second causes. And though he ordinarily concurs with second causes according to the law given and order set, yet sometimes there is in his providence a variation and digression. Though he has given creatures power to act; and man, to act as a cause by counsel, and has furnished him with active abilities; yet he has not made any creature master of events; but reserves the disposal of issues, and events to himself. Herein the absolute sovereignty and dominion of God appears.

2. Otherwise, the Lord might possibly suffer real disappointment, and be defeated of his ends in some instances. He might be crossed in his designs, if any of his creatures could do what they will, without absolute dependence upon him. He could not be sure of his ends, and what he designs in the world, if he had not command of all events that may further or hinder them. If there were any active power in creatures that he cannot control; or any one event that is out of his reach, and absolutely in the creature's power. Exempted from his providential command, it would be possible that he might be defeated of his ends, and so far unhappy, as to his voluntary happiness, which results from his having his glory in the world, and compassing all his ends in the works of creation and providence. God has made all things, works all things, and manages all things according to the counsel of his will, in a way of subservience to himself, and his own occasions. Which he could not do universally and completely if he had not the absolute and infallible determination of all events in

his own hand. "But his counsel shall stand, and he will do all his pleasure," (Isa. 46:10).

So much for the explication, and confirmation of the doctrine.

Part 5: Of Instruction – Use 1

1. We see what a poor dependent, nothing-creature proud man is. Depending absolutely on God for his being, actions, and their success. Men of greatest sufficiency cannot get their own bread, or bring anything to effect in their own strength. Let their abilities be what they will, (swiftness, for the race; strength, for the battle; wisdom, for getting their bread, *etc.*), yet they shall stand them in no stead without the concurrence and blessing of God. Man says, he will do this and that. But he must ask God leave first. He says, today or tomorrow I will go to such a place, and buy and sell, and get gain. Where he does not know what shall be. But it shall certainly be as the Lord will. The way of man is not in himself, it is not in man that walks to direct his steps, nor perform any thing that he purposes, without divine concurrence, or permission. He does not have the success of any of his actions in his own power; nor does he know that anything he does shall prosper. One would wonder how poor dependent man should be so proud! Any little thing lifts him up. When the soldier on such occasions as these, is in his bravery, in his military garb dressed up for the purpose, with his buff

coat, his scarf, his rich belt, his arms, a good horse under him, O! what a goodly creature is he in his own eyes! And what wonders can he do in his own conceit! And yet he has as absolute need of God's assistance, if he goes forth to battle, as any naked, unarmed man he cannot move a step, or fetch his next breath, or bring his hand to his mouth, or leap over a straw, or do anything, without help from God, "in whose hand his breath is, and whose are all his ways," (Dan. 5:23). It's strange to see how the hearts of men are lifted up with nothing! O! cease this from man. For in which is he to be accounted of?

2. We see that there is, and there is not chance in the world. There is chance in respect of second causes. So, some things fall out as our Savior speaks in Luke 10:31, "And by chance there came down a certain priest that way: and when he saw him, he passed by on the other side." But this is not chance as to the first cause. That piece of atheism, and heathenism ascribing things to fortune and chance, is hardly rooted out of the minds of men, that are or should be better instructed and informed. The Philistines, when they were plagued, could not tell whether God had done it, or a mere chance happened to them, (1 Sam. 6:9). They did not understand that what was a *chance* to them, was *ordered* by the

providence of God. Truth is, chance is something that falls out beside the scope, intention, and foresight of man, the reason and cause of this may be hid from him; and so it excludes the counsel of men; but it does not exclude the counsel and providence of God; but is ordered and governed by it. And it is so far from being chance to God, that there is as much (if not more) of the wisdom, and will, and power of God appearing in matters of chance and contingency, as in any other events.

 3. We see here something of the power, and greatness, and glory of God appearing in his efficiency, by which he works all in all. As he is himself independent, so all things have an absolute dependence on him. He gives success, or causes disappointment, as he pleases. So that men are wholly beholden to him for all the good they enjoy. For victory, for bread, for riches, for favor and acceptance, for all. Nothing comes to pass without his permission, if it is moral evil; without his concourse and cooperation, yes, predetermination, if it is moral or physical good, or penal evil. In *him* we live and move, and have our being. The counsels of the ablest statesmen, no matter how rational, shall not prosper without him. Ministers, no matter how sufficient, pious,

learned, industrious, zealous, shall convert no man, edify no man, comfort and establish no man, *without him,* (1 Cor. 3:6-7). Though Scholars study hard, they shall make no proficiency without the blessing of God. The merchant may trade, and project rationally, and yet shall not grow rich on it, unless God gives him success. It is God that makes, "Zebulun rejoice in his going out, and Issachar in his tents," that crowns the labors of seamen, merchants, and husbandmen with success. "Except the Lord build the house," *etc.,* (Psalm 127:1).

Training days, artillery days, those of great use, and very necessary, yet, are all in vain, unless the Lord blesses them. He must instruct, and teach, and accomplish you; otherwise the help of your expert officers, and your own endeavors to learn war, will signify nothing. And when valiant soldiers come to fight; whatever skill, a strength, and courage, and conduct, and advantages they have, yet, they will be worsted, if the Lord does not give success. We should learn from this to admire the power and greatness of God. It is a lamentable thing, that he that does all, is thought to do nothing! He can work without means, by insufficient means; and blast the ablest instruments. And yet is little minded in the world. God gives forth a challenge to idols, "do good, if you can, or do evil," (Isa. 41:23). It is God's prerogative to do good or evil, *i.e.* not the evil of sin (which argues defect and impotency; and does not come within the compass of omnipotence to do it) but of punishment. God only can give good, or award bad success, and reward or correct and punish his creatures that way. "Who is he that saith (what man or angel?) And it cometh to pass, when the Lord commandeth it not?" (Lam. 3:37). O! see, and adore the greatness of God in this respect! He works all in all.

Part 6: Of Instruction – Use 2

A word of terror to the enemies of God, even all impenitent and unbelieving sinners. "Woe unto the wicked, it shall be ill with him. For the reward of his hands shall be given him," (Isa. 3:11). Their persons, and works, and ways are in the hand of God. That God whom they despise, disobey, and rebel against, disposes of them, and all their times and chances; and, "who ever hardened himself against him, and prospered?" (Job 9:4).

Let me tell you briefly, that either 1. You shall be unprosperous men, that nothing shall succeed well with you, as it is said of Coniah, "write this man childless, or bereaved (of posterity, lands, and goods) a man that shall not prosper in his days," (Jer. 22:30). Or, 2. You shall prosper to your hurt. The successes you have, shall undo you. A godly man may be unsuccessful in the management of his affairs; but then his ill success succeeds well to him; humbles him, weans him from the world, does him good. His soul prospers by means of his unprosperousness. But your successes and prosperities make you proud, insolent, bold to sin, hardhearted, atheistical, and more rebellious against God; and further your eternal ruin, (Job 21:7-15), because they have no changes (but a constant, even, uninterrupted course of prosperity) therefore "they fear not God," (Psalm 55:19).

Or, you shall prosper, not for your own sake; but for the good of others, Job 27:16-17, Prov. 13:22. And the final issue of all your ways and actions, and the concluding event that will befall you, if you persevere in a course of rebellion against God, will be most dreadful. In this life, one event may happen to the righteous, and the wicked, (Eccl. 9:2). But the last general great event that shall befall them, shall be very different. For the event shall be, that the righteous shall be saved and the wicked damned. This shall be the portion of the cup of impenitent wicked men, and the event that shall be ordered out unto them by the Lord, that they shall be cast, both soul and body, into hell. He that determines all events, will at last put a sad issue to the prosperity of his enemies. They must needs be very unfortunate, and unhappy men at last, that persevere in rebellion against him that governs time and chance according to his pleasure.

Part 7: Of Instruction – Use 3

A word of singular encouragement to the dear people of God, that have an interest in God through Jesus Christ, and walk with him according to the tenor of the covenant of grace. All your times, and chances, and changes are in God's hands; and all that befalls you, is under his management, and of his ordering, and disposal. Then, "Say to the righteous, it shall be well with him. For he shall eat the fruit of his doings," (Isa. 3:10).

God will give you the fruit, the benefit, the success, the good event of all your gracious counsels, and undertakings. He that has the master and ruler of events on his side; must certainly do well. Though you are weak, and insufficient, in yourselves, to do duty, to walk with God in your course, to resist temptations, yet the race is not to the swift, nor the battle to the strong. God can, and will prosper your sincere endeavors, and give in suitable supplies of strength and grace, (Isa. 40:29-31). And though you have many enemies; sin, Satan, the world, and the flesh, and may meet with much opposition, yet God that has all issues and events in his hand, being on your side, nothing shall do you real hurt, (Rom. 8:31). You do not need to fear what men, or devils can do against you, seeing God that manages the active power of the creature, is for you. They have no power, except what God gives and hands to them as he will, (John 19:10-11), and he will not suffer them to do you real hurt, "Nothing shall separate you from the love of God in Christ, (Rom. 8:35–39). No, all adverse powers, though they are of greatest sufficiency to do you any hurt, and are bent on it, shall do you *good*, whether they want to or not, (Rom. 8:28). And you shall be sure to conquer at last and have good success. Indeed, you may at present have many particular designs and undertakings, and be frustrated and suffer disappointment in it. But then, it is good for you to be afflicted, crossed, disappointed; and unsuccessfulness is really best for you, and most conducive to the prosperity of your souls; and you shall be sure of good success, so far as infinite wisdom sees it to be good for you. And then, however your particular designs and undertakings may be defeated. Yet, you have a general grand design, that is paramount and predominant; which is the everlasting enjoyment of God. And if you reach that, you are well enough, and as happy as you would be. And the Lord, who is the Lord of time, and disposer of events, and Governor of his creatures to their ends, will not suffer you to be disappointed herein. You shall infallibly glorify God and enjoy him forever. This is a matter of comfort to the people of God in the worst times; when it is with them as with Jacob, when he said, "All these things are against me," (Gen. 42:36). When none on their side, refuge fails, and no means appearing for them. And indeed, the people of God in this country have had great experience of this. What deliverances has God commanded! When few, and weak, and low, and exposed to the rage of enemies, God said, "...touch not my anointed, and do my prophets no harm."

The salvations of New-England have been most apparently by the Lord's governing time, and chance. This or that chance or occurrence has fallen in in the very nick of time to prevent ruin. It has not been from the sufficiency of the instruments of our salvation; but from the all-sufficiency of God, and his overruling events wonderfully, therefore, let all that fear God, comfort themselves with this consideration. And that you may take down, and be refreshed with this cordial, consider two things. 1. That events are not to be judged or concluded of beforehand, from the aspects of second causes. As astrologers conclude this or that shall happen, because of this or that aspect, the conjunction or opposition of planets, and posture of the stars and heavenly houses. So, politicians do this from the prospect they take of the combinations and confederacies, and various aspects of second causes. Here, also, God's people are discouraged, when they see the world combine, and enter into leagues and confederacies against the church; now they conclude they shall be a prey to their teeth, and swallowed up. And enemies are ready to insult over the church, and to say as Pharaoh, "I will pursue, I will overtake, I will divide the spoil," *etc.*, (Exod. 15:9). But this is a wrong way of judging, because time and chance happen, and God may turn all a quite other way. It was a good observation of Mr. Joseph Caryl, "When wicked men are nearest their hopes, godly men are furthest from their fears." This is because, then, usually God defeats them; and their insolence, and confidence engage him to do it.

3. That the determination of all events, is in the hand of God in Christ, or of the Lord Jesus Christ. The Mediator is at God's right hand, and has all power in heaven, and earth committed to him; all judgment, and the command and government of all events. He governs time and chance. God is in Christ providentially ruling all events; prospering, or blasting all affairs, as he will. It

is the Man upon the throne above the firmament, that gives out his orders, according to which the living-creatures (or angels) move the wheels of providence, as you may see in that excellent scheme of providence, which is drawn in the first chapter of Ezekiel. And it's well for believers, that themselves, and their works are in the hand of Christ, and that all events in the world are determined by him. That Christ, whose person you love, whose ordinances you love; whose truth you love whose commands you love; whose members you love; whose appearing you love. That Christ, that loves you a thousand times more than you can love him, and loved you above his own life, and will love you to eternity, that blessed Lord Jesus Christ has the managing of all affairs, and of all your concerns and undertakings in his own hands. And, therefore, we may conclude that he will do all in favor of his members, and it shall be well with them that fear God, (Eccl. 8:12).

Part 8: Of Exhortation – Use 4

1. Labor to maintain a humble sense of your own insufficiency to accomplish anything, even in that kind in which you seem to be most sufficient and best accomplished. Let worthy magistrates in consultations for public good; ministers, in their ministerial way; scholars, in their way, and soldiers, in their military capacity, *walk humbly with God.* Truly God has poured contempt on our military men, our artillery men, and good soldiers, New-England has gloried in these things, indeed, men of martial spirits and skill, ought to be encouraged. These trainings and exercises are very commendable, and by all means to be supported and countenanced. And it is pity that as in other things, so in this, the good old spirit is so much gone. These are not times in which the nations beat their swords into plough-shares, and their spears into pruning-hooks. War, in some cases is lawful, and at sometimes necessary; and sure then, learning of war is so also. But I fear we have trusted too much in sword and bow, and gloried in our numbers; in our arms and ammunition. In our trainings, in our expert soldiers. And the Lord has shown us, that all these things are nothing without his

blessing. And that unless the Lord watch the town, keep the garrisoned house, fight the battle, all is in vain. We have seen that a despised and despicable enemy, that is not acquainted with books of military discipline, that observe no regular order, that do not understand the soldier's postures, and motions, and footings, and forms of battle; that fight in a base, cowardly, contemptible way, have been able to route, and put to flight, and destroy our valiant and good soldiers. And I must confess, that which determined my thoughts to this text, was this very consideration. I do not know whether my discourse on it may seem so well leveled at the occasions of this day. But I know it is very proper for the times that have passed over us, and the dispensations thereof. And I hope the gentlemen-soldiers present will not blame any of us, if we cannot look upon their trainings, and artillery-exercises with such an eye as formerly before the war. No, they are to blame themselves, if they do not look on them with another eye themselves, considering how God has humbled us in that respect. Whether my discourse is pertinent to the day or no, yet I am sure, it is a lesson God has been teaching of us by many sad defeats and overthrows by a despicable enemy, that the battle is not to the strong, or expert, or valiant; nor success always answerable to the sufficiency of instruments; but determined by the Lord, ordering time, and chance according to his pleasure. It is plain, that the Lord has spoken this over and over in his providence, and it is very proper for the dispensers of the word to speak it after him, and inculcate the same humbling lesson. Nothing's more apparent, than that God's design at this day, is to humble magistrates, our worthy patriots, to humble ministers, churches, expert and valiant military-men, merchants, and husbandmen, all sorts of men among us. Who does not see that God's design is to humble proud New-England? Therefore, I admit, and beseech you, in this humbling discourse in an humbling time and suffer this word of exhortation, the drift which is, not to discourage you from the use of means, or take off your edge from military exercises; but to press you to get and keep a due sense of your own insufficiency in your several capacities, to do any exploits, or accomplish any good purposes of yourselves. And may there not be need of a humbling word on such days as these, when there are such solemnities, and the hearts of poor men are ready to swell, and heave, and be puffed up strangely, with great apprehensions of themselves? Well, be sensible of your insufficiency to effect anything, whatever your wisdom and strength are. That you cannot of yourselves, win the race, or battle; get bread, or wealth, (Deut. 8:17-18). You cannot build the house, or keep the city, (Psalm 127:1-2). Truly we had need to be put in mind that we are but weak, sorry men, that cannot make our own fortune; but must take what God orders out to us.

2. Depend *absolutely* on God for all the issues and successes of your affairs and undertakings. For you see their determination is in his hands. Though wicked men would shame the counsel of the poor people of God (deriding their course in this respect) because they have made God their refuge (as Psalm 14:6) yet, do not be ashamed of your dependence on God, nor either jeered, or affrighted and discouraged out of it. It makes for the glory of God, as well as your comfort, when you depend upon him. Therefore, (1.) Make sure that all your counsels and undertakings are lawful and good. Otherwise you cannot duly depend on him, and expect his gracious concurrence. Indeed, God may shine on the counsels, and way of the wicked, in respect of outward prosperity. And so, he may give you success in wrath, and for your greater hurt, when your undertakings are

sinful. But you have no promise of his gracious concurrence in that case, to ground faith upon.

(2.) Do what your hand finds to do, with all your might. As in the verse before the text, "Be not slothful," or neglective of duty, because of the uncertainty of events. Though you do not have the issue in your own power, yet you are to do your utmost towards the compassing of your lawful designs. Do your duty, or you cannot expect God's blessing, and his determining events on your side. Great complaints there have been from time to time of the neglect of these military exercises, even by those that have freely listed, and solemnly engaged themselves to attend them; and that such days are spent away unprofitably, little done to any purpose; as if they were days to meet on, to smoke, and carouse, and swagger, and dishonor God with the greater bravery and solemnity. O! make a business of it, and not a play. And in all your lawful undertakings, be serious and diligent. Uncertainty of events should not hinder from duty and diligence, (Eccl. 11:6).

(3.) Renounce all confidence in creatures, or created sufficiency. The Psalmist says, "I will not trust in my bow nor shall my sword save me," (Psalm 44:6). Do not trust in great men (they are a lie, (Psalm 62:9)).

Good men, any men, they are vanity. Do not make flesh your arm, nor lay too much weight upon the ability of any instruments. Do not bear too much upon the sufficiency of ministers to instruct, convince, convert, comfort and edify. For Paul himself was nothing, (1 Cor. 3:6-7; 2 Cor. 12:11). Do not say, wisdom and strength are for the war (as Isaiah 36:5). And in this we will trust. For events do not always fall out accordingly. Do not let the "strong man glory in his strength, nor the wise man, in his wisdom, nor rich man, in his riches; but in the Lord," (Jer. 9:23-24). Do not trust in your own wit, art, strength, courage, military accomplishments, provisions for war, advantages, or any sufficiency you have. Do not trust in any qualifications you have, natural or acquired, civil or spiritual. Do not trust to the sufficiency of received habitual grace. When God said to Paul, "my grace is sufficient for thee," he does not mean only habitual grace, but actual, efficacious, assisting grace that the Lord was pleased to afford him, the *epichoregia pneumatos*, additional supplies of the Spirit, and supplying as well as created grace, which Paul was to trust to, and so might glory in his infirmities, and depend upon the power of God that rested on him, (2 Cor. 12:9-10). Do not trust to your previous dispositions and preparations, for any duty. It is not in him that wills, or runs. Take heed of self-fullness, and a spirit of independence in this respect. Self-confidence, and creature-confidence are inconsistent with a due dependence upon God.

(4.) Beg good successes, and issues of your undertakings of God, in the name of Jesus Christ. It is one of the characters of a good soldier, (Acts 10:2). And I am sure it is of a good man, to be a man of prayer. It would be well if all our artillery and military gentlemen were men of this character. It is well if none of you have come forth to day without solemn prayer to God for his blessing on the occasions and services of this day. Some read those words in Isaiah 36:5, "Thou sayest, surely lip-labour is counsel and strength sufficient for the war." As if Rabshakeh flouted good Hezekiah for his confidence in God, and for saying that prayer (which he scoffingly calls words of lips, or lip-labor) would be instead of the best policy, and courage, and preparations for war. But if this reading is somewhat forced, yet it is sure, that although prayer to God must not exclude the use of other means (for how can a man pray in faith, that does not also use all due means in his power?) to get the victory, and win the day. Therefore, when you come to these exercises, beg military skill of God. And when called forth to real service, beg success of him. So, in other cases, prayer is one of the best expedients. Our Savior has instructed us to pray for our daily bread. Scholars should beg a blessing on their studies. *Bene orâsse est bene studuisse.* So, for favor and acceptance among men, beg so much as may put you into a better capacity to do the work of your place, and serve your generation. When Paul was to carry a liberal contribution to the poor saints at Jerusalem (which was like enough to be very welcome) he begs the romans to strive together with him in prayer, that his service might be accepted of the saints, (Rom. 15:30-31). Pray, therefore, in the name of Christ, for the good success of all your lawful undertakings. In this you will express your dependence on God.

(5.) Cast all the care of events and issues of your affairs and undertakings, on the Lord. Use all the good means in your hand, and then leave events quietly with God, on whom all the issues of things depend. "Commit your way to the Lord, and roll it off thy self upon him," (Psalm 37:5). Look to him to direct "thy paths to a good issue," (Prov. 3:6). When you have done your duty in the use of means to compass your lawful designs, and recommended all to God by prayer, then trouble yourselves no further; but "cast your burden upon the Lord," (Psalm 55:22; 1 Peter 5:2). Take that counsel, Phil. 4:6, it is our work to take care our duty to be done, and the Lord's work to take the care of events. It was a brave speech of that gallant soldier, though none of the best men, I mean Joab, when he had set his men in battle array, and used all the skill and policy he could, "be of good courage, and let us play the men, for our people, and for the cities of our God. And the Lord do that which seemeth him good," (2 Sam. 10:12). We must not govern the world. Nor encroach upon God's prerogative (which is to dispose of events) by taking the care of them on ourselves. Be poor and weak in your own eyes, and commit yourselves and concernments to him.

(6.) When you have in this way done this, then believe steadfastly that the Lord will give you a good issue of your undertakings. It may not be that which you may desire; yet that which is best for you. When you have the greatest sense of your own insufficiency, and the weakness of means; yet believe this, and depend on him for it according to his promise, with whom it is all one to save by many, or few; weak, or strong, to convert and edify by weak, or able ministers; to feed his children, and make them look fair and fat, with pulse and mean fare, as well as with royal dainties. Depending on God like this, excludes presumption on one hand, and despair and discouragement on the other. And he that in the sense of his own insufficiency, trusts in the power and grace of God, may say as Paul, "When I am weak, then am I strong," (2 Cor. 12:10).

Oh then! Let us depend upon God, with whom are the issues of all affairs. Let our honorable rulers depend upon him, in the management of public affairs. Let ministers depend on God, without whom they cannot instruct the ignorant enlighten the dark, convince the obstinate, awaken the secure sinners, convert and bring any souls to Christ, gather Israel, edify and build up the faithful in the knowledge and faith of gospel mysteries, and in the graces and consolations of the spirit. Let merchants depend on God for prosperous voyages, and good success in their trade and commerce. Let husbandmen depend upon God for their bread and livelihood more than upon their own labors, and the fruitfulness of the ground. God instructs the husbandman in Isaiah 28:26, "and blesseth his labors," and can soon blast them, as the experience of many years has sadly taught us. Let scholars depend on God for learning, more than upon their books, or tutors, or parts and industry, or any other advantages. Let military men learn to depend upon God, "the Lord is a man of war," (Exod. 15:3). He gives military skill, and other accomplishments, and successes also in their services and hazardous undertakings. Let us all learn this lesson, to depend on the Lord, that orders out all successes and events according to his pleasure.

3. Duly acknowledge God in all successes and events; and in all frustrations, and disappointments.

First, acknowledge God in all good successes and events, so as to be thankful to him for them. Whatever your own sufficiency may be, yet acknowledge God thankfully, as if you had been wholly insufficient. For your sufficiency is of God, and he could have disappointed notwithstanding. The ground of our unthankfulness for all good issues and events of affairs and undertakings, is, because we do not see the good hand of God dispensing all to us. We make too little of God, and too much of our selves; either by thinking we deserve better than God has done for us (here a proud heart is never thankful to God or man) or by thinking we have done all, or more than we have done, toward getting this or that mercy. We put ourselves too much in the place of God; as if it were in our power to make our endeavors successful, and to give a good effect and issue to them, according to our desire. We get up into God's throne, and usurp upon his prerogative, and assume that which is peculiar to him, when we presume we can bring anything to pass, or do anything successfully in our own strength. If we make our selves the only and absolute first causes of our good success; no marvel we make our selves the last end also, and deny God the glory. Oh do not ascribe good success to your own wit, and parts, and policy, and industry, and say, my nimbleness has won the race; my conduct and courage has won the battle; my wisdom has gotten me this bread; my understanding has heaped up this wealth; my dexterity, and skill, and complaisance, and agreeable conversation has procured me the favor of rulers or people; my parts or study has given me this learning. Do not say with the vaporing Assyrian, "by the strength of my hand I have done it, and by my wisdom. For I am prudent," (Isa. 10:13). Do not let this be so much as the secret language of your hearts. Do not say, as Nebuchadnezzar, "...this is great Babylon, which I have built," and so derogate from God that works all in all; lest he turn you to grazing like a beast in the field, as he did him, even with the beasts of the field, and teach you better manners by some severe correction. Do not, "sacrifice to your own nets, and burn incense to your drags; as if by them your portion were fat, and meat plenteous," (Hab. 1:16). Instead, ascribe all to God. There is that deep wickedness in the hearts of men, that if they get anything by any fraud, and crafty fetches, and overreaching of their brethren, in a sinful way, they will be too ready to attribute that to the providence and blessing of God, and say, it was God's providence that cast it in on them; when they have been craftily and sinfully designing it, and bringing it about. But when they have gotten anything honestly, by their wisdom and prudence, and industry, they are too ready to forget providence, and ascribe all to themselves. See the evil of this, and remember that no people in the world have greater cause of thankfulness than we have to God, who has governed time and chance on our behalf marvelously. O! bless him for good success, not only when you cannot but acknowledge your own insufficiency; but also, when you have apprehensions of the greatest sufficiency of second causes. And, "blessed forever be the Lord, who has pleasure in the prosperity of his servants," (Psalm 35:27).

Secondly, acknowledge God also in all your frustrations and disappointments, so as to resent his disposals and dispensations towards you in a gracious manner. We have met with many disappointments in the late war, and in other respects. We should see God in everything. When he blasts our corn, defeats our soldiers, frowns upon our merchants, and we are disappointed; now acknowledge the hand of God, ordering time, and chance according to his good pleasure. Justify God in all, and bear such frustrations patiently. When you have done your duty, be quiet, though the event does not answer your endeavors, and hopes. Take heed of quarrelling at God's disappointments. Do you know whom you have to do with? "I was dumb, I opened not my mouth; because thou didst it," (Psalm 39:9).

If we look at faulty instruments, or only at mere chance, we shall be apt to murmur. It is the observation of one, that the reason why men are more apt to fly out into cursings and blasphemies for their bad luck (as they call it) in those unlawful games of cards, and dice, than in other exercises, that are governed by art and skill, arises partly from the very nature of those games.

Because when they have tried their lot or chance over and over, and their expectation is deceived, they think that that power that governs the lot or chance, is adverse to them. They cannot blame their own art or skill, when no art can infallibly determine the event; but curse their bad fortune. And if we look at disappointments, as only our bad fortune and chance, looking no further, we shall be apt to fret and quarrel. But if we do indeed see God ordering our lot for us, it may and ought to silence us. When magistrates have done their duty, according to the law of God, and of the country, and endeavored faithfully to give check and stop to the inundation of profaneness and heresy; and yet the bad genius of the times, and ingenious humor of the people, and this or that emergency happens, that frustrates the success of their counsels and endeavors; truly they may sit down and mourn indeed; but yet humbly submit to the all disposing providence of God. When ministers have labored faithfully, and yet Israel is not gathered, and their labors seem to be in vain, not successful in converting sinners; they may weep in secret indeed; but yet patiently bear the unsuccessfulness of their ministry from the hand of God. When soldiers have showed themselves valiant, and faithful, and done what they can;

and yet are vanquished. They must acknowledge God's hand in it, and that, "the battle is the Lord's," (1 Sam. 17:47). It is God who governs the war, and determines the victory on what side he pleases. All men have briars and thorns springing up in the way of their callings, as well as husbandmen, and meet with difficulties and crosses in it. Get the spirit David had (2 Sam. 15:25-26), and so acknowledge God in everything, as to submit humbly to his disposals, even when they are adverse, and cross to your desires and expectations.

Thirdly, be always prepared for disappointments. Do not promise yourselves success from the sufficiency of second causes. God may determine otherwise. We should be forewarned and forearmed, that we may not ξενίζεσθε (1 Peter 4:12) *think it strange* when it comes to pass, or be dejected and discouraged. Events are not in the creature's power. The Lord sometimes disappoints men of greatest sufficiency, overrules and controls their counsels and endeavors, and blasts them strangely. Time and chance happen to them. If Adam had stood; though he would not have had the determination of events and successes in his own hand, yet God would have determined them for him according to his hearts-desire. And he should never have been disappointed. But since the fall, as no man has power to determine events (which is God's prerogative) so it is just with God that every man should meet with crosses and disappointments; and this is the fruit of the curse, under which all natural men are. And as for the people of God; though they are delivered from the curse of the law, in its formality, so that nothing befalls them as a curse, how cross it may be, yet they are not yet absolutely delivered from the matter of the curse, as appears by the afflictions they meet with, and death itself. And indeed, it makes sometimes for the glory of God, to disappoint men of the greatest abilities. When men do not see and own God, but attribute success to the sufficiency of instruments, it's time for God "to maintain his own right" (as Dr. Preston speaks) and show that he gives, or denies success, according to his own good pleasure. God is much seen in controlling the ablest agents, and blasting their enterprises; yes more, many times, than in backing them, and blessing their endeavors in an ordinary course of providence. In this the wisdom of God is much seen. It is best that it should be so with respect to God's interest and glory. His power also appears in giving check to the ablest instruments, and turning all their designs another way than they intended. His mercy also to his people, is seen herein; for it is best for them, in some cases, to be defeated and disappointed. His justice also appears in this, in his correcting and punishing the self-confident, sinful creature with unexpected disappointments. So that it is our wisdom, to look for changes and chances, some occurrents and emergencies that may blast our undertakings, that faith and prayer may be kept a going, and lest if such frustrations befall us unexpectedly, we either fly out against God, or faint and sink in discouragements. At the first going out of our forces, in the beginning of the war, what great apprehensions were there of speedy success and ending of the war; that it was but going and appearing, and the enemy would be faced down. As if the first news from our soldiers should be, *venimus, vidimus, vicimus.* And several times after, great probability of concluding that unhappy war; and yet all disappointed, contrary to expectation. When there is therefore the greatest probability of success, yet remember there may be disappointment; and provide for it, that you may not be surprised thereby. This may be good counsel to men of projecting heads, that are wont to be very confident that they see their way far before them. But they do not know what time and chance may happen. This may check the confidence of man, and teach us not to promise ourselves great things, or build upon this or that event or enjoyment for time to come. Labor to be prepared and provided for disappointments.

Part 9: Conclusion

Fourthly, "fear God, and keep his commandments. This is the conclusion of the whole matter," Solomon says, (Eccl. 12:13). The conclusion of the book, and may be very well drawn from the words of my text in special, and shall be the conclusion of my discourse upon it, "fear God, and keep his commandments."

Oh! Fear God, that is the Lord of time, and Governor of chance, and dispenser of all events and issues; and be sure to please him in a course of evangelical obedience. God has the care of events, and we must leave that to him. But our care must be to do our duty. And, to fear God, and keep his commands, in the whole duty of man. "Who would not fear thee, O king of nations?" (Jer. 10:7).

The Lord governs nations and kingdoms, all the affairs and enterprises of the sons of men. All their lives, and souls, and estates, and ways are in his hand. And he can dispose of them, not only for present, but for eternity, as he pleases. All the events that be fall them, are ordered and governed by him. Therefore, be in the fear of the Lord all the day long, and walk worthy of the

Lord unto all well-pleasing. If your ways please God, your enemies shall be at peace with you, or do you no hurt, if they would; but good, whether they will or no. Obedience is the best way to prosperity, (Deut. 29:9). The Lord takes pleasure in the prosperity of his servants, (Psalm 35:27). This was God's promise to Joshua, (Joshua 1:8). While you are with God, God will be with you, (2 Chron. 15:2), and then you shall have things prosper under your hands, as (Gen. 39:23). Everything shall befriend you. While Solomon walked in the steps of his father, and walked in the law of God, and neither practiced idolatry, nor gave any countenance, or allowance, or toleration to it, there was no adversary, nor evil or chance. For it is the same word with that in my text, 1 Kings 5:4, when he forsook the law of God, the Lord stirred up many adversaries against him. While he was with God, his affairs prospered, and were attended with good success and a blessing. So it was with reforming Hezekiah, (2 Kings 18:5-7; 2 Chron. 31:20-21). He trusted in the Lord God of Israel, so that after him was none like him among all the kings of Judah, nor any that were before him. "For he clave to the Lord, and departed not from following him; but kept his commandments which the Lord commanded Moses.

And the Lord was with him, and he prospered whithersoever he went forth," *etc.*

Otherwise, how should men expect to prosper? 2 Chron. 24:20, "why transgress ye the commandments of the Lord, that ye cannot prosper? Because ye have forsaken the Lord, he has also forsaken you." We find generally that when rulers and people walked in God's law, and kept in with him, their affairs prospered marvelously. When they departed from God, nothing prospered with them; unless it were to their hardening, and ruin. And the Lord keeps the same tenor of dispensations (for the substance) to this day. Oh therefore! Let us all account it our best policy, as it is our duty, to please God, that has the absolute disposal of us, and all our affairs. And let it be the care of our military men, that they do not make days of training, and preparation for war and real service, days of provocation to God. Please God, if you would engage him on your side, to govern time and chance to your advantage. Take heed of making God your enemy in the days of your peace and of such solemnities, by spending them away idly and unprofitably, by any unworthy behavior; by intemperance, by excessive drinking (a sin grown too much in fashion with the generation that is risen up; I wish I might not say, with many loose church-members) by idle, rotten, unsavory communication, or by any other way of debauchery, and provocation. So as to disarm yourselves, to make you naked, to lay you open to the stroke of divine vengeance, and to render you unprosperous and unhappy men in all your undertakings. It is a shame and a grief to think how such days as these are many times spent to the dishonor of God, and the unspeakable prejudice of the souls of men; as well as other days of solemnity on other accounts. I implore you, look to yourselves, and do not make war on God this day, nor, "run upon the thick bosses of his bucklers," (Job 15:25-26). Do not dishonor and displease Christ, that is God the father's viceroy in the world, and governs all affairs. If you cross him, and (to speak after the manner of men) disappoint him of his expectations concerning you (as the Lord has great expectations of such a people, so circumstanced) he will have his time to meet with you, and to cross you in your designs, and to give you shame, and disappointment. I do not delight in any pedantic, insipid, trifling allusions, below the gravity of a sermon. But I cannot better express what I would, than in your own ordinary phrases, you gentlemen of the artillery, and militia, face to your

Part 9: Conclusion

leader; or in the apostle's words, "look unto Jesus," (Heb. 12:2). And follow your leader, your commander in chief, the captain of the host of the Lord, (Joshua 5:14). The Lord Jesus Christ, in holiness of conversation. He was no glutton, no wine-bibber, no loose and vain companion of sinners; though blasphemously charged with it by his malignant enemies. He was the greatest example that ever was, or will be in the world, of sobriety, of gravity, of seriousness and diligence in his work, of prudent and prosperous management of his affairs (Isaiah 52:13), of savory, gracious communication, and holy conversation. Learn of him, and follow his example, and you shall be prosperous men indeed. Yes, let us all take this counsel and course. New England has enemies enough on earth, and in hell. Woe to us if we make God in heaven our enemy also. The Lord help us to fear him, and keep his commandments, and then we do not need to be afraid of evil tidings, or solicitous about events and issues of things. For all the paths of the Lord shall be mercy and truth to us, and goodness and mercy shall follow us all our days. And this we know, that it shall be well with them that fear God.

FINIS

Other Helpful Works from Puritan Publications

God's Sovereignty Displayed
by William Gearing (1625-1690)

A Christian's True Spiritual Worship to Jesus Christ
by Stephen Charnock (1628-1680)

The Efficiency of God's Grace in Bringing Gain-Saying Sinners to Christ
by Simeon Ashe (d. 1662)

The Two Wills of God Made Easy
by C. Matthew McMahon

A Treatise of God's Free Grace and Man's Free Will
by William Perkins (1558-1602)

The Largeness of God's Grace Seen in Predestination
by William Perkins (1558-1602)

The Good Which Comes Out of the Evil of Affliction
by Nathaniel Vincent (1639-1697)

www.ingramcontent.com/pod-product-compliance
Lightning Source LLC
LaVergne TN
LVHW041549070426
835507LV00011B/1001